The Last Africans

The Last Africans

The original edition was published in 1977 under the title "Die letzten Afrikaner"
by Perlinger Verlag

1st edition 1977   1–30 thousand
2nd edition 1978   31–60 thousand
3rd edition (fully revised) 1981   61–90 thousand

© 1978 Perlinger-Verlag Ges. m. b. H., 6300 Wörgl (Austria), Brixentaler Strasse 61
Photography, text and layout: Gert Chesi
Drawings: Rudolf Kreuzer
Reproduction: Wagner'sche Univ.-Buchdruckerei, Innsbruck
Produced by Welsermühl, Wels (Austria)
Printed on Euroart 150 g/m² by Borregaard
No part of this publication may be reproduced in whole or in part without permission in writing
from the publisher
ISBN 3-85399-002-9
Printed in Austria

Contents

Preface

This illustrated volume, "The Last Africans", portrays in a rich and colourful manner a cross-section of indigenous and unadulterated West African culture. This culture, which is reflected in the social organization and way of life (music, dancing, art, clothing, rites, architecture) of the rural African peoples, has been given vivid and living expression in this unique book. As the title of this book correctly suggests, the rich culture of the black continent is in danger of becoming extinct. Recent history has had a detrimental effect on this culture, and it is still suffering from the aspirations of its present leaders and its peoples.

Colonization by European powers and Christianity, which was forced onto the African people, initiated a process of cultural alienation and extinction in Africa. The exploitative nature of colonialism sought to create, for its own selfish ends, a new African in the image of European values, and Christianity almost succeeded in suppressing and replacing the indigenous religious forms which, to a large extent, represented the roots and life source of the expression of much of African culture.

Another major factor which has contributed and continues to contribute to this process of cultural alienation and demise on the African scene is that of development and modernization. This has come about in the post-colonial era with the creation of new states and with it the introduction of modern education, economic planning systems and industrialization. This process of development and modernization, which may be mandatory and essential for the economic viability and survival of the newly independent African states, will, in the foreseeable future, continue to have a tremendous, disintegrating effect on traditional African values and culture.

"The Last Africans" prophetically anticipates this tragic but probably irrevocable trend and seeks to document the rich tradi-

Professor Francis K. Nkrumah and Gert Chesi during an interview.

tional way of life and culture of Africa before they become adulterated or, even worse, disappear altogether. At the same time, this book tenders a subtle warning to the new generation of Africa that we may be in danger of destroying forever what makes us truly African. In this respect, it is somewhat encouraging to note that some African leaders and nations have come to realize this danger and have sought through various institutions to recapture past traditions and to encourage the projection of the "African personality".

However, "The Last Africans" reminds us that time is not on our side and that a much greater effort is needed to preserve our rich African cultural heritage. If Africa must progress and modernize, and it is in its interest to do so, the foundation for modernization and advancement should be based on the framework of its rich social and cultural background.

Francis Nkrumah

Professor Francis K. Nkrumah

The Situation of the African now and in the Past

For the past couple of centuries alien civilizations have been infiltrating African life, thus influencing the evolution of the African, who, within an extremely short period of time, has had to undergo a process of development which lasted for centuries in Europe. With the commencement of trade, alien cultures began to force their way into Africa. Missionaries arrived, colonialism set in, and the alien sphere of influence grew and has continued to grow to this day. The African was never able to make his own decisions but always had the will of others forced upon him and this led to the gradual disintegration of his independence. All of a sudden his cultures and religions were jeopardized, and massive pressure from outside crippled his personality, forcing him to give way to new ideologies and concepts.

Unlike the European the African is totally dependent on the soil for his livelihood. His survival depends on nature, and the forces of nature are therefore an important part of his life, of his religions. He regards the prosperity of his crops and his herds as an expression of divine approval, and he tries to retain this approval by making sacrifices. He believes himself to be weak because he is human and cannot exercise divine influence, without which his life would be inconceivable. This is why masks are such an essential element of his religions. He believes that the mask will enable him to break through his human bonds and to adopt a new personality, that of an animal or a demon, at the same time relinquishing the old one. He believes that the mask will give him the power of influencing the course of nature and that the ritual will give him the opportunity of doing so.

Sexuality is also a very important part of African life, not only because it serves to maintain the species but also because it is regarded as an expression of divine power which takes hold of man for a moment, lifting him above the limits of his human bonds, allowing him to become one with nature in a climax he can normally only reach after a ritual dance when he falls into a trance. Many African religions are founded on the belief that man is the product of a union between heaven and earth.

Through ancestor worship it is also possible to contact the gods, for it is believed that when a man dies he sets out on a journey to the gods and can then ask them to fulfill the wishes of his descendants. When he has been dead a long time he finally reaches a place next to the gods from where he himself can guide the destiny of his descendants. The worst disaster would be for an African to annoy his ancestors who would take revenge by inflicting the family with disease, famine and death.

At the beginning of the nineteenth century missionaries appeared on the scene and, in their ignorance, began to preach a religion which must have been completely incomprehensible to the average African. And what was worse was the fact that the African was not given a choice in the matter. Because he was so completely dependent on the missionaries and the colonial powers he was forced to adopt this new religion.

His dependence has, in fact, been his undoing. Even now, after the era of colonization, economic ties have remained intact making it possible for alien powers to infiltrate the very core of Africa with their ideologies. The various Churches have been joined by huge companies whose policies will eventually tempt the African into the world of consumption thereby destroying the remnants of existing traditions.

Take, for example, the concept of economic aid to developing countries. Its very wording is misleading. Several well-meant projects do exist; most of them, however, will eventually change the very foundations of African life. The would-be aid is really nothing more than the possibility of exchanging a rural life in freedom for a proletarian one at the assembly line.

The past few decades have witnessed a rural exodus and the development of huge cities and large sprawling slums. Lured by the improvement in living conditions an industrial society would allegedly provide, people were tempted to leave their village homes for what they thought would be a better life in a big city. Prosperity, however, materialized for only a few, the majority was doomed to live in the slums of cities like Abidjan or Lagos. In Dar es Salaam, for example, the police discovered that more than fifty people were living in the basement of a single house. Far from solving any of Africa's old problems, urbanization and civilization have created completely new ones. Whereas Abidjan prides itself for having opened Africa's first children's village, Lagos is at a loss to know what to do with its high crime rate.

Our so-called civilization is also about to destroy the African's attitude towards his family. A few years ago an African would not have known what an orphan is, for in traditional Africa there was no such thing. Orphanages were non-existent and completely unnecessary because the family was there, and the family was responsible for the welfare of the children. The same applies to old people's homes. In a country where ancestors were honoured as gods it was completely inconceivable for old people to be rejected; the family was responsible for them as well. The tribe's responsibility for the individual was not considered a nuisance but a duty which was performed with respect and as a matter of course.

Then the first Europeans began to arrive bringing new problems with them. Not that life had been a paradise before: Tribal struggles, disease and famine had made life difficult enough. But the problems Africa now faced were completely new: strange diseases, wars and exploitation, not to mention the sectarians, preachers and missionaries who forced the Africans to adopt new religions, depriving them of their old ones and leaving them uprooted. The old rituals were replaced by a new liturgy, and ties which once had been strong were severed. The influence of the family began to crumble, and the tribe, which had once been responsible for the survival of the weak and the sick, began to disintegrate. A European form of society took its place and to this day it has not been able to adapt itself to the peculiarities of Africa.

Europe has never tried to understand the rituals and customs of other civilizations, nor the reasons why they exist. When travellers, for example, brought home tales of the cruelty of African initiation rites, hardly anybody attempted to find out whether the cruelty of the rites was justified or not.

Part of the initiation rites of the Fon in Benin or also of the Somba, is for an adolescent to throttle, roast and then eat his dog. Cruel as this custom may seem to us, it has a reason. For an African the essence of sacrifice lies in giving up something one loves, a living thing to which one ist attached and whose death will leave its mark. Our religions also judge penitence and sacrifice according to the degree of effort involved. The moral value of a dog sacrifice is therefore greater than that of a sacrifice which is neither an economic nor a spiritual loss for the one who is making it.

The Mofu in Cameroon sacrifice a bull to their ancestors. The bull is often fattened for years in advance and its loss is difficult to bear, for the Mofu themselves can only afford to raise goats and hens and it is almost impossible for them to buy another bull. The greater the sacrifice, the higher its value—and if one takes this into consideration one begins to understand how wrong it is to regard rituals such as initiation rites in the course of which dogs are sacrificed, or ancestor worship involving the sacrifice of a bull merely as the crude acts of a primitive people.

Rituals involving self-inflicted pain are not acts of pointless cruelty, but have profound meaning. During the initiation rites of the Somba, for example, the young men whip themselves and although this ordeal is an extremely painful experience, it creates very strong ties because it is shared by all the young men taking part in the ceremony. The same applies to the Senufo, whose laws require that those who have been initiated together help one another in times of extremity. The psychology behind these rituals can be compared to that of European soldiers who have experienced war together and, regardless of origin or ideology, feel bound to one another years later because of their common fear of death. One of the aims of African initiation rites is therefore to create ties which are able to survive decades and which will hold strong in times of extremity. And these rites were used again and again as an excuse for destroying African religions and cultures.

In Africa a man's value is not judged according to his efficiency or his ability to work hard but according to his attitude towards his tribe, and, after all, Europe is a good example of how many efficient and hard working criminals society is capable of producing. Freedom is relatively unimportant, it is what commits a man to his tribe, his behaviour within the social structure of this tribe as well as his courage to meet the forces which threaten tribal existence that determine his value as a human being. If a man leaves his tribe to look for work in the city he is considered to have failed in his duty towards his tribe. He is trying to escape from the commitments involved in leading a traditional tribal existence, where humility and loyalty to the tribe are of such immense importance. Traditional Africa regards work for the sake of prosperity alone as a lack of modesty and a weakness in character.

Nevertheless, thousands of people have left and continue to leave their villages to look for work in the factories of the big cities. Slums on the outskirts of these cities have been the result because there was not enough work for everybody. And this is not all: Crime and anti-social behaviour such as prostitution in the European sense of the word or the rejection of unwanted children have been another tragic consequence of this development.

One of the first things one notices when in Africa is the tremendous poverty of the people. But is it really poverty or are we just judging the situation from a European point of view, and is what we consider to be poverty actually a form of contentment completely unknown to us? Europeans have never really been able to understand the African nor, until recently, have they ever attempted to comprehend the complicated patterns of the African way of life. Even in the nineteenth century, long after the Europeans had begun to settle in Africa, the natives were believed to live in trees, to practice cannibalism and to be very stupid and slow. This view was held until a very short time ago because the Europeans were not at all interested in the people themselves but only in the exploitation of Africa's natural resources and labour. The only interest the European had in the African was one of placing him at the service of the white man, and if he could not be sold as a slave, his labour was bought at as cheap a price as possible.

This attitude has influenced the whole course of African history and can still be observed today. Most economic aid is regarded as an investment which will eventually yield a profit, and most African countries are still dependent on Europe and America, only now the dependence is an economic one.

A few centuries ago Europe showed very little interest in Africa. In the Middle Ages an exploration of the continent was out of the question. The endless Sahara lay in the north, and it was impossible for ships to sail around the rocks of Cape Bojador in the west. The east was under Arab control, and a very barren and inhospitable area anyway, and so it was impossible for Europeans to progress southwards.

It was known that the Arabs had trade relations with the Africans, and that the Egyptian queen Hatshepset had made a successful expedition to Punt (now Mozambique) as early as 1493 B.C. However, Africa remained for centuries a legendary and unconquerable continent, a continent regarded with ignorance and prejudice. In Europe, people who had never even been to Africa wrote books about the country. The African was thought to be little better than an animal. The existence of an African culture was categorically denied, and the African was considered to be a primitive, sadistic creature whose only means of expression was brutal fetishism and pagan idolatry. The Europeans, in their complete ignorance, took heed of outward appearances only, failing utterly in understanding the meaning of what they saw.

The standard of culture in the Sudanese kingdoms of Ghana, Mali, Songhai and Kanem-Bornu during the Middle Ages was comparable to that of Europe. Around 1500 the book trade was the most important branch of trade in Timbuktu, and travelling merchants reported that the city, which had a population of 40,000 at the time, was a city of scientists and scholars. The East African city of Malindi was a prosperous trading metropolis, and Vasco da Gama was amazed to find a civilization there, equal to that of Europe.

After the first successful circumnavigation of Cape Bojador in 1433, the Portugese set up trading posts all along the west coast. Their first settlement was Elmina in what is today Ghana. Twenty years later they had established several such trading stations, even in the Congo, and it is an interesting fact that Portugal even sent an ambassador to the court of the Manikongo, the ruler of the Congo, offering him economic aid. Portugal then sent masons and carpenters to build his palace and they were followed by missionaries who converted the king and some of his retinue. Later, however, after delegations had been exchanged, the king severed the ties of friendship with the Portugese, and his heir refused to allow them to continue their development program.

In the course of time the African tribes were often on the move, and although we know very little about their movements it is possible to follow their tracks because of the recurrence of certain rituals and stylistic peculiarities in their art. It seems that the Yoruba, who now live in western Nigeria and parts of Dahomey, once lived in Egypt. Their masks and statuettes as well as their customs and traditions obviously contain Egyptian elements.

Even Christian elements were incorporated into some black African religions, the result being hybrid customs, some of which have survived to this day. One of these hybrid religions was that practiced by the Bwiti in the jungles of Gabon. This sect was originally founded by the Mizogo. In 1927 the Fang reorganized it and it is a good example of the effect the missionaries had on black Africa. The Bwiti practiced a highly unchristian religion using Christian symbols, candles, rosaries, crusifixes and altars. The rituals involved blood sacrifice for the purpose of exorcising disease or cursing enemies.

15

African art is essentially different from European art in that its creativity is the product of the artist's religious beliefs and philosophies. When an African takes up his carving tool, he does so because he wants to please the gods, to protect himself from spirits and demons, or to create a new abode for the wandering soul of his ancestor. Every detail has a special meaning founded on tradition, and art for the sake of art alone is practically non-existent. This also applies to music, architecture or any other creative activity.

The African world of spirits contains a great variety of evil one has to protect oneself against, and art is a perfect way of conversing with the spirits. For example, the *Kanaga* mask of the Dogon, who live in the area south of the Great Niger Bend, protects the hunter from the spirit of the animal he has killed. It is a mask of atonement and is supposed to have been made by the first hunter, who set out to kill the mythical bird *Kanaga.* Another kind of mask is the hare mask which also serves to protect the hunter from the revenge of the dead animal.

African religions have had a great influence on the development of African art which derives its meaning from these religions. This is why Christianity and Islam had such a disasterous effect on African art, causing its degeneration and adulteration. The ignorance and intolerance of the Europeans in Africa hastened the process. Even men like Albert Schweitzer were not interested in African art. On the contrary, they tried to put a stop to it because they realized that by furthering it they would be sanctioning its meaning, its religion.

Unless the European is prepared to disregard his European aesthetic taste when estimating the worth of a mask or statuette, he will never be able to understand African art. The African has no word for the concept of beauty. A work of art can be good, an expression pertaining to its quality and the purity of its style, but mainly to its ability to frighten off demons or to personify the ancestors. It can be good, but not beautiful, and this is one of the reasons why so few Europeans ever find access to African art.

The Kirdi

The home of the Kirdi is northern Cameroon, the area between the Nigerian border and the banks of the Logone. They are a good example of the terrible degenerative effect tourism and religious and political upheavals can have on the culture of a tribe. Christianity had little influence in this area. Mohammedan teachings had a much stronger impact, managing in no time, with the help of various political hegemonies, to destroy the spiritual and traditional backround of a whole tribe.

In the early Sixties René Gardi travelled through the Mandara Mountains and was impressed by the virginity of the area and the manifold cultures of its inhabitants. The Kirdi had always been an unpopular minority, dominated and repressed by the Moslem Fula. This and the contempt with which they were met by the other, more powerful tribes proved beneficial for their traditions, enabling them to maintain their spiritual heritage until a very short time ago. They were considered too stupid to lead a civilized life and being of no use as soldiers, they were simply forgotten. Today the Kirdi are still despised, even though they have absorbed much of the Fula civilization. According to the Sub-Prefect of Meri, a Fula would never sit at the same table with a Kirdi. The word itself is a term of abuse, Kirdi meaning the godless one or the unbeliever.

A lot has changed, however, in the last couple of years. Even marginal minorities have felt the impact of a rapidly spreading development. State resettlement projects were organized to move the population of the mountain areas into the plains, so as to improve the infrastructural situation. Epidemics broke out and were followed by inoculation campaigns which made it possible to gather statistical information about the Kirdi. Then tourist agencies began to offer package tours to the Mandara Mountains which meant the end of a forgotten people. Mohammedan politicians declared nakedness a crime and crowds of tourists shamelessly abused the last remnants of their freedom. Because they had to wear clothes, they stopped wearing jewelry and the traditional leather skirt, the "Cache-Sex". They exchanged their beautiful beads for miserable rags which are always torn, dirty and full of vermin. And thus a tribe was clothed in clothes it had never wanted because it had never seen any need for them.

The Kirdi number approximately 200,000 people who are divided up into more than forty smaller groups. Most of them live in the Mandara Mountains, a few of them in the plains and on the banks of the Logone.

For may years the Kirdi were a persecuted minority. The slave trade of the Fula caused them to be either dispersed or assimilated by other groups. The same thing happened to the tribes of the southern Adamaua Plateau. It was the German colonial rule that finally put a stop to the slave trade of the Fula.

As is the case with all peoples of the savanna, the Kirdi are also masters of ritual and cult. Ancestor worship dominates their life. Every dance, every festival is religious and serves to improve relations with the dead. In some ceremonies the ancestors are worshiped even more than the gods.

19 War dance of Kirdi men. – 20/21 The Mandara Mountains near Cape Siki, the home of the Kirdi. – 22 (above) A Cape Siki farm south of Mokolo. – 22 (below) Kirdi houses near Mora. – 23 A Mofu farm near Meri. – 24 Phallic silos near Meri. – 25 Millet farmer of the Mofu tribe constructing a silo. – 26–29 War dance of the Mofu. – 30 A Kirdi mother with her children wearing the "Cache-Sex", the traditional costume of the region south of Mokolo.

The most important festival of the Mofu and the Matakam, relatively small Kirdi tribes, is the *Maray* festival, or the Festival of the Bull, as Jean-François Vincent calls it. The Mofu of Meri celebrate it for about a month. Only when the chief of one massif has made his final sacrifice can the festival be celebrated in the next one. It is celebrated in honour of the dead, and the sacrificial bull is often fattened for years in advance. Only few have the right to sacrifice a bull and a man is only entitled to do so if his father has already sacrificed one. This time schedule is based on the recurrence of the festivals which follow each other in strict order. After the Maray, but in the same year, the festival of the young *Mazgala* is celebrated. In the course of this initiation ceremony young men between the age of 16 and 20 are received into the world of adults. Throughout this festival, which lasts for a couple of weeks, they are obliged to wear festive attire and serve the chief. At each of the following two *Marays* they are given new titles, new attire and new offices. It is only in the course of the third festival, when they are 28 to 30 years of age, that they are declared to be mature men. However, they are still not entitled to sacrifice a bull. After they have taken part in six *Marays* they are permitted to sacrifice a bull if they can meet the necessary requirements. By now they are 48 to 52 years of age. The people believe that disaster will descend upon the tribe if the sacrifice is unsuccessful or if the complicated ritual is disturbed, for carelessness might annoy the ancestors to such an extent that they would take revenge in the form of disease, fire or famine. This is why every effort is made to secure success because then the ancestors are obliged to protect the family and to ward off catastrophes.

The last *Maray* was held in 1972 and it is doubtful whether another one will ever take place. For one thing, only a few of the Mofu can afford to fatten a bull; the only animals they normally keep are goats. And apart from this the consumption of European goods has proved too great a temptation. Their traditions are slowly but surely degenerating, and scenes which in the Sixties were part of everyday life are now already part of history. It was

31

apparent decades ago that the African cultures would eventually die out, and in the last couple of years, with the help of European industrial products, this has really come to pass. The plastic bag has replaced the leather pouch; clothes from various European charities are worn instead of leather strips and fringe skirts, and the bow harp, which until a couple of years ago was an essential part of all cultural activities, lies forgotten in a corner, its place having been taken by the popular transistor radio.

Whenever the Kirdi smith "cooked" iron, forged ploughs or poured small phallic medallions for use in rituals, he never did so without a musician at his side, playing the bow harp to the rythm of his hammer. Any procedure the people considered to be supernatural had to be treated with respect. It was therefore only natural before beginning any ritual to make a sacrifice to the gods in order to win their favour. The people respected nature and her forces, and music, sacrifice and prayer were therefore essential. It was this philosophy of life that also shaped the people. Respect for the aged and tribal ties were part of African tradition, a tradition Western civilization is about to destroy.

With a bellows of goat leather, air is blown through a clay pipe into the furnace. When the furnace is opened, the lumps of iron which have formed at the bottom can be removed.

33 Matakam farm in the Mandara Mountains. – **34–37** During an annual festival the Mofu dance in honour of their gods. – **38–40** War games without bloodshed are a part of every festival. – **41** Elderly women paint their faces with red clay. – **42/43** Kirdi smith sacrifices a hen. – **44/45** This loom looks ancient but in an expert's hands it can produce wonderful materials. – **46** Vessels for the dead souls. – **47** A Kirdi child wrapped in goatskin is carried to a festival.

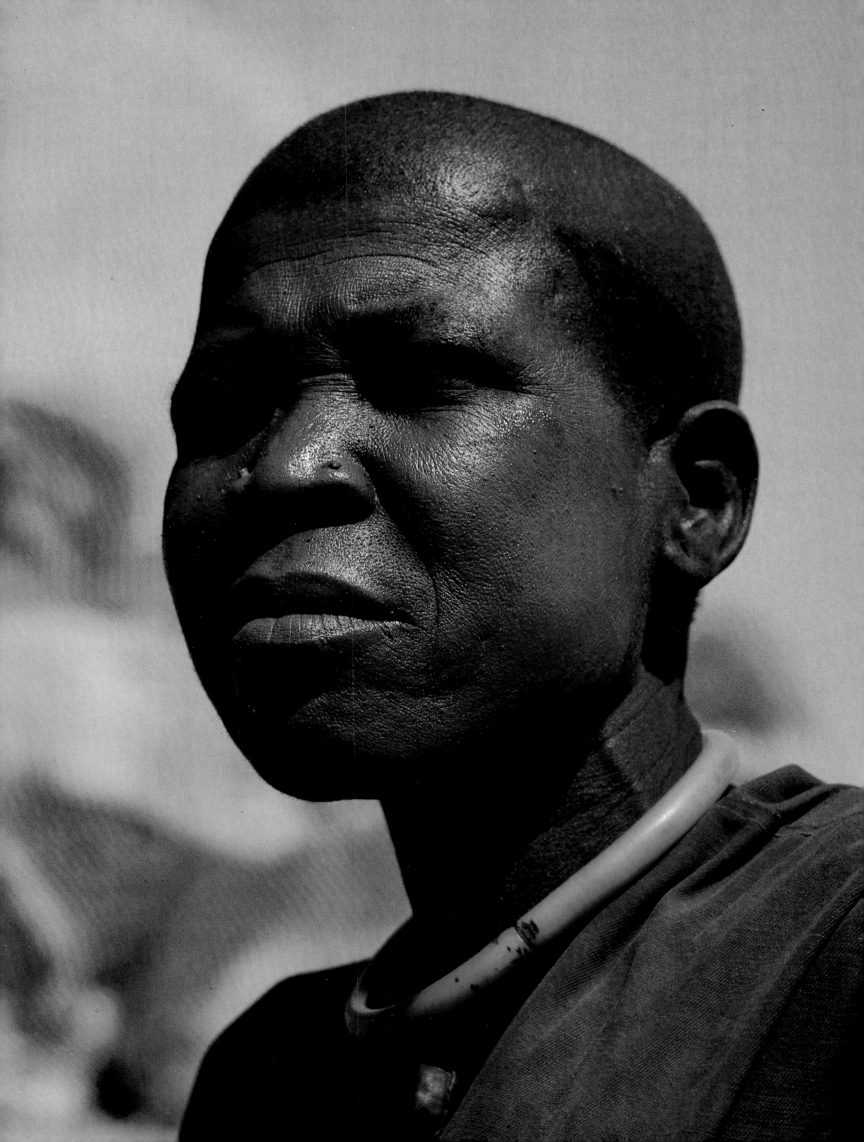

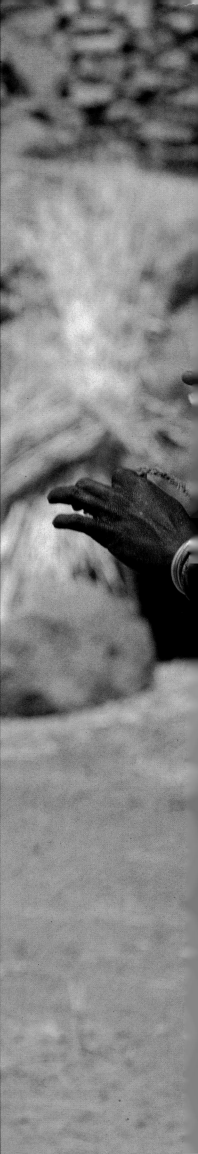

The Ashanti

Hardly any other African tribe can look back on such an affluent and turbulent past as the Ashanti. Theirs is a history of violence and wars. They are famous for the ignominious part they played in the slave trade and we also associate their name with gold, which for centuries was of such vast importance for trade on the west coast of Africa. They have a highly developed culture and their society is rigidly organized.

Until 1957 Ghana was officially called the Gold Coast. Long before the first European appeared in Africa, the Arabs traded in Ashanti gold, transporting it via Timbuktu or Agadés to the Mediterranean coast. The situation changed, of course, when the Portugese landed on the West coast. The gold trade shifted its axis and until large gold resources were discovered in America most of the gold worked in Europe came from Africa. The Ashanti culture was founded on this gold which became an essential part of their social and religious life.

One of the most famous Ashanti kings was Osai Tutu, who lived in the early eighteenth century. He was a great warrior and had a tremendous influence on the future destiny of the Ashanti people. With arms bought from the Dutch, who had established trad-

49   **48** Ashanti funeral ceremony at Kibi.

ing stations along the coast, he conquered several relatively small kingdoms in the north of the Gold Coast. In 1719 he conquered Akwamu, after having subjected Gonja, Banda, Dogomba and Bono. This enabled the Ashanti people to move south, towards the coast and thus towards the source of future wealth.

One of the most important characters in Ashanti mythology is a priest by the name of Komfo who was an advisor to King Tutu. According to the legend, Nyame, the god of the sky, commissioned him to make the Ashanti a great nation, and in proof thereof gave him a stool of gold. This stool became a symbol of power and was handed down from generation to generation, gradually becoming the object of intense religious feeling. The people believed it to symbolize their ancestors, and their king, who owned all the land, became their spokesman.

The Golden Stool has always been an important symbol for the Ashanti because it unites them as a people: Each person, each family, each village community is part of the Ashanti nation; each dogma and each religion is part of the Ashanti religion. And, as a symbol of unification, it has even aquired political significance.

When in 1900 Sir Frederic Hodgson demanded in the name of the English colonial government that the Golden Stool be brought to him, a revolt broke out among the Ashanti, followed by a war over the Golden Stool. What the English obviously did not know was that it was regarded as containing the soul of the whole nation, and if it were captured or destroyed the Ashanti would perish. Nobody, not even the Ashanti king, was permitted to sit on the Golden Stool.

Whereas in almost all African societies property is considered a form of avarice, the Ashanti attach such importance to material wealth that they go as far as to display their private treasures in public. It is therefore customary to display the gold and jewelry of

50 The Okyehene, the king of Kibi, at the funeral ceremony of his predecessor. The grass in his mouth symbolizes the fact that it is forbidden to speak during the ceremony. – **52/53** Scenes during a funeral ceremony.

the family during various festivals. The family's social standing depends on the community's assessment of its wealth and the greater its social reputation, the larger its collection of gold and jewelry.

The possession of gold has always been the privilege of the Ashanti kings. There used to be a law according to which every lump of gold exceeding a certain size had to be delivered to the Ashantehene. The people were only allowed to possess gold dust,

54, 55, 58, 59 The Okyehene of Kibi (Ghana) is carried to the funeral rites of his predecessor. After the death of an Ashanti king there are several of these celebrations which can last up to seven days. Drummers and dignitaries who accompany their "chiefs" come from the neighbouring villages to pay their homage to the dead king. In former times such festivities were an occasion for human sacrifices. The skulls of those killed still adorn the drums of the musicians today. Their music is considered to be a dialogue with the gods.

which became the basic currency and was also used for making gold weights, which are very much in demand today.

It is a surprising fact that although European institutions have firmly established themselves in the Ghana of today, the old traditions have remained intact in the form of rituals. It may seem strange for the Ashanti dignataries and leaders of today to arrive at the various festivals in modern cars. However, during the ceremonies, far away from any alien civilization, they are still the true representatives of the old Ashanti nation who, as in the days of King Tutu, still regard themselves as an inseparable entity.

55   **56/57** Kibi during the funeral celebrations which last for a week.

Kumasi is the political and intellectual capital of the Ashanti kingdom but neighbouring areas such as Kumawu or Kibi have also brought forth great rulers who, in keeping with their traditions, have had a great influence on the religious, social and political affairs of their people. In November 1975, the Okyehene of Kibi and his followers celebrated the anniversary of the death of his predecessor. Four months later he himself died.

When a new king is elected the king's mother inaugurates the election in her capacity as the owner of her own Silver Stool. First of all she must consult the elders of both families from which the king is descended and then the chosen king is made known to the other elders of the town. As soon as they have agreed upon a successor, his name is made known to the popular assembly, con-

58

vened especially for this purpose. It is only then that the people are asked for their approval. The festive enstoolment of the new king then follows. In the course of this ceremony the elders admonish the newly chosen king to be a good ruler of his people and he swears to this before the goddess of the earth and the ancestors of his tribe.

Although the power of the Ashanti king is great, the social hierarchy contains certain democratic elements not even he can ignore. One of these institutions is the *Mmerante,* an association of men, which on certain occasions sends representatives to the king with requests. Another one, the *Abusua,* represents the maternal

60/61 The Ashanti are considered experts at lost wax casting.

clan and mediates between the individual and the clan. At marriage ceremonies the *Abusua* guarantees with a certain sum of money the loyalty of the wife. Should she become unfaithful, the *Abusua* has to pay the sum of money promised to the husband. To ensure that this should not happen, all the members of the *Abusua* watch over the marriage.

The Ashanti believe their neighbours, mainly the Denkera and the Techiman, to have invented the gold weight. The goldsmiths have always been responsible for the production of scales and weights, but also of other equipment such as shovels. They were the only craftsmen who were able to understand the many complicated symbols with which they decorated the weights. They also devised several thousand proverbs which were then embodied in small yellow brass objects. Figures, tools, animals and fruits, but also various groups of objects were used to illustrate a proverb. The motifs and forms were varied in a thousand different ways and often encoded. Many weights have been found representing ancient tools and instruments and through them it has been possible to discover forgotten elements of a rich cultural past.

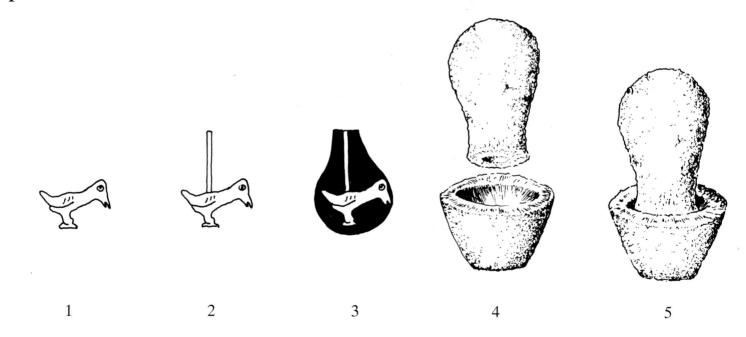

1   2   3   4   5

This sketch illustrates the working process of lost wax casting from the model to the finished cast. Figure 1 shows the wax model. (2) The wax stem which later serves as the ingate is added. (3) The wax model is embedded in carbon. (4) This is then given a clay casing and put into a crucible. The wax model is melted out. In the crucible there is the metal which is to be smelted.

The Ashanti did not only make gold weights but also beautifully made casts in so-called lost forms and they developed this art to perfection. Such casts are still made in the same fashion today, only now the weights are no longer in use and are therefore not standardized.

The peoples of the west coast have known brass and bronze for centuries. A model of beeswax, which for the larger models has a core of sand, is embedded in a clay form. When it has dried, the clay form is heated and the wax is melted and poured out. Small animals, beetles, crabs or plants used instead of beeswax are burnt out of the clay casing and thus a hollow arises which is then filled with brass or bronze (see sketch).

Although gold dust lost its value as a currency in 1889 – at that time only English currency was accepted – gold has still retained its importance, particularly for religion. When a temple is consecrated, it is decorated with gold like every new fetish shrine. At burials rulers or dignitaries are decorated with gold dust. Gold dust wrapped in a piece of cloth has also retained its significance as a grave offering.

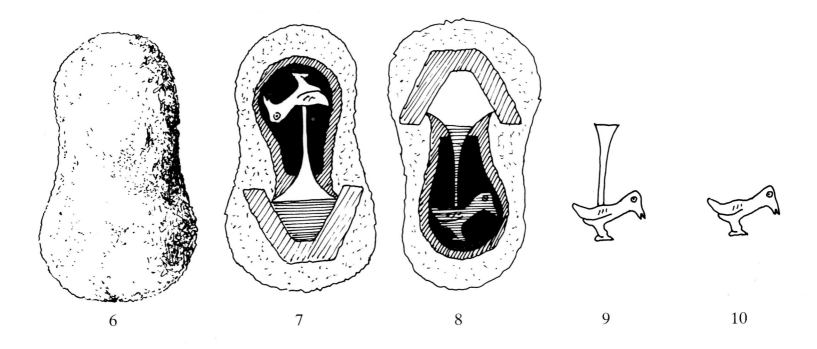

6   7   8   9   10

(5) The crucible and the form are then held together by a clay casing (6). In the furnace the mould is heated and the metal is smelted. (7) If the form is turned round (8) the liquid metal flows into the hollow. (9) After smashing the form, the blank emerges with the metal stem of the ingate. (10) The cast is then cleaned; the ingate spot is filed smooth and polished.

63

The Bororo

The endless savanna south of the Sahara is the home of the Bororo. It is a country demanding the utmost of man: deprivation, exertion and a will to survive even if years of drought should reduce the cattle to skin and bones, if sand storms should hide the sun for days on end or continuous lack of nourishment endanger the lives of the children. This is the life of the Bororo, a unique people, believed to have been among the first inhabitants of Africa, the descendants of the mysterious people of an ancient era who sculptured fantastic drawings into the rocks of the Tibesti Massif or the Tassili Mountains thousands of years ago.

The Bororo are a small group of nomads belonging to the Fula, a tribe which can be found in the area between Senegal and Chad bearing various names, the most common of which are Fulbe, Peul, Pullo, Fulani or Fellani.

The nomadic life they lead has shaped them. Carving and moulding were arts practiced mainly by sedentary farmers and the creative expression of the Bororo has been restricted to their jewelry, their dances and the magnificent manner in which they paint their bodies. They have developed this art to perfection and, incited by their tremendous desire for beauty, have created magnificent

65

64 Bororo woman of Niger in the jewelry she normally wears.

masks and devised elaborate patterns which they paint onto their bodies.

The men are delicate creatures and at annual competitions they hold hands and recite poetry. They differ completely from their neighbours, the Kirdi, who express their virility in wild competitive games and violent rituals. The inconsistency in the Bororo way of life becomes apparent on the day after a festival when they can be seen standing at a water-hole surrounded by their herds and their enormous bulls or wandering untiringly from pasture to pasture. No other tribe in Africa has such a strong relationship to its herds as does the Bororo. Their animals are a part of everything they do, think or feel.

Our search for the Bororo began in Niger. We travelled from Agadés to Tahoua, following their tracks through the savanna and dunes south of Abalak, picking our way carefully through dry river beds and thorny shrubs, slowly moving along the path leading to the small station Permu, the home of Parade, the chief of the Bororo. We pursued their herds from one watering place called Igu to another called Issu and discovered pastures where hundreds of cattle and goats graze. The Bororo are among the last Africans to lead lives completely unaffected by the progress of civilization. They still respect the laws of nature and their ancient traditions, and this helps them to survive even in an area as extreme as this. Their lives are ruled by one desire–the desire to be free and to roam wherever nature may lead them.

In December, after the rainy season, the grass begins to wither and the sun grows warm. It is then that the Bororo move south to where they can still find some water and enough grass on which to feed their herds. The season of their festivals and rituals does not begin until the rain falls in May. The men then sit around in small

67 Bororo in North Cameroon. – 68 Bororo youths in festive attire. The beauty of the men is a matter of great importance to these Nomads. – 69–75 The Bororo women also value jewelry and like to be well-groomed. The brass ornaments they plait into their hair have to be polished every day. – 76/77 Pools covered with water lilies are the drinking places of the Bororo herds after the rainy season. – 78–81 Even the children work hard at the wells to ensure that there is enough water for the herds. – 82 Youths confer with each other before the dance begins.

66

groups and paint their faces. This is the time when their three great passions become evident: their passion for beauty, their herds and their families. It is, however, also the season for courting. They perform a traditional dance called the *Yake*, whereby they re-enact the hierarchy, the social structure of the tribe. The young men stand in a group in the middle surrounded by adolescent boys. All of them have taken stimulating drinks and have painted their faces with ochre and antimony powder. Then the dance begins. They dance with delicate and graceful movements, passionately but without aggression. The girls approach the dancers and shyly indicate which one they prefer. This custom is derived from a legend in which the young Bororo Chedan is said to have seduced his sister Golle. Chedan marries her before anyone realizes that she is pregnant and flees with her into the bush. This legend is the reason why, from time immemorial, Bororo youths have decorated themselves and dance a dance of seduction during which the girls choose the man they think the most handsome.

Andrew Baring describes another dance in which the youths throw spears into the air, turn round and catch them again. This feat is aimed at impressing the girls, who give prizes of turbans and clasps to the most skilful dancers.

When two young people have found each other at the festival, the complicated ritual of courting begins. The young man goes to the parents of the girl and brings them a calabash of milk. Only after they have agreed to the marriage does he return to his family to fetch three oxen, which he brings to his parents-in-law as the price for his bride. After the animals have been slaughtered, a feast begins and the whole clan joins in.

Depending on the size of his herd, a Bororo can have several wives. Should one of them be unfaithful, the betrayed husband challenges his rival. They then fight with knives, sabres or clubs until one of them is injured. The wounded man complains to his chief who then starts a great palaver.

There are various theories about the origin of the Fula. One of them claims that they are of Judeo-Syrian descent and that they

83

reached Senegal and the Sahel region via Egypt. During their migrations they are thought to have interbred with the Berbers. Three waves of migration can be traced, one of which crossed the Libyan desert; rock paintings found in the Tibesti Massif are proof of this theory. The second reached Macina via the Algerian oasis Adrar and the third roamed through Morocco and Mauritania as far as the Great Niger Bend.

A second theory claims that the Peul are of Hamitic origin and that they were very influential in the Sudan and Upper Senegal. At the end of the thirteenth century they migrated to northern Nigeria. Today the Peul are separated into several groups. Some of them have become sedentary and have even settled in towns. They call themselves Fulbe Siire and, in the eyes of the nomadic groups, they are traitors because they have voluntarily relinquished their freedom which is of such importance to the Peul. In the last couple of years the Sahel region has been receiving more and more economic aid which, due to lack of research on the part of the helpers, has often had the opposite effect to what was intended. Mechanical waterpumps have suddenly made it possible to convey large amounts of water for much larger herds than before. The consequences of this have been negative: Excessive pasturing has totally destroyed the sparse grass supply and the heavy hoofs of the cattle have caused large areas to become karstic. Apart from this the groundwater level has sunk to such a degree in some areas that the few trees that used to grow there have also died. In addition to this, extensive irrigation projects which aim at industrializing cattle breeding have been taken into consideration. The Peul, who would no longer be needed as herdsmen, would be able to find work in leather factories.

If these plans are ever realized, the European spirit of enterprise will have destroyed yet another unique culture, thereby taking advantage of a nation which for thousands of years has lived in freedom and independence.

85 On the path leading to the watering-place. – **87–95** The men, who have put make-up on for the festival, wait for the girls to arrive.

Building in Africa

In the last couple of years well-known scholars and architects have begun to show an interest in the phenomenon of anonymous architecture. The architecture of primitive peoples, in regard to both form and content, used to be considered merely the product of geographical and climatic conditions. For a long time both their sacred and their profane buildings were denied any creative individuality. Recent studies by Paul Lebeuf have given new access to architectural phenomena which he maintains are a fantastic synthesis of religious, political, social and cultural necessities. Studies of the Dogon, the Fali and the Somba show that African architects have always had to adapt their work to innumerable mythical and symbolic systems as well as to the spheres of power of various age groups, the economic and political system as well as the overlapping of Islamic and animistic conceptions. Apart from this the African has his own concept of form and space, which, more than is the case with any other race, is directed towards man and his needs. African architecture does not only incorporate all these basic elements, it also reflects even the smallest units of African society, such as the family.

African society distinguishes between various groups: sedentary farmers, nomadic herdsmen, hunters and collectors. For each of these groups architecture serves a basically different purpose: The farmer builds a strong and solid house; the hunter constructs a temporary shelter which he soon abandons; the dwelling of the nomadic herdsman is movable and he also owns furniture and utensils which are of great importance to him—everything he owns

96 Tellem dwellings from the twelfth century. Till today the dead of the Dogon are still buried in these caves. – **98–101** Hausa villages in Niger. – **102/103** Farm in northern Ghana (Sirigu). – **104** (above) A clay building in Nigeria. On the roofs paprika are dried. – **104** (below) Basket-like granaries in Niger. – **105** The mosque of Agadès. – **106** Living quarters near In Gall (Niger). – **107** (above) Living quarters and (below) silos in Niger. – **108/109** Musgum houses in North Cameroon.

must be light in weight, detachable and movable. Whereas the Bororo let their women build grass houses they then fill with the furniture they have brought with them, the Tuareg carry their tent-like houses around with them. These have roofs made of many strips of goat leather sewn together, and the whole house can be easily set up or dismantled.

The Dogon build according to strict, religious plans. Their architecture is marked by total subordination to the existing religions and traditions. The fishermen of Ganvié, however, have settled in lake dwellings which answer both their economic and their social needs.

This rich array of African architecture has now reached a point in its historical development when it is being superseded by other alien styles of architecture. At the beginning of the colonial era, the so-called colonial style was predominant. Today modern European architecture is gradually replacing it. Whereas the European style of building was reserved for the colonialists, it is the governments of the young independent states that are now supplanting the traditional forms with new materials and styles. During the French occupation of Cameroon, the Musgum were granted subsidies, and so they were able to continue building and cultivating their dome-like houses. The African politicians who followed have, more or less, stopped granting these subsidies so that the decay of traditional building has mercilessly set in.

Cross-section of a Musgum farmstead (Cameroon).

Strong economic interests have led to the development of large tracts of land. This and the efforts to move the African out of the bush have resulted in the steady decline of African cultures. Modern settlements have frequently turned into slums because they lack the organic arrangement and the fundamental spirit characteristic of African villages.

Cross-section of a Mofu farmstead with phallic granaries (Cameroon).

The Buildings of the Kirdi

The architecture of the Musgum or Mofu is less dominated by religious or spiritual aspects than is that of their neighbours, the Fali, whose mythology is reflected in their architecture. This is especially true of the Fali who live in the plains. Those who live in the mountains, as do most Kirdi groups, are more independent in their building, adapting their farms to the needs of the moment. Their buildings are round, the roofs are cone-shaped and they are built very close together on the slopes of the mountains. This is because these regions are so densely populated and the area suitable for cultivation is so limited. This has led some to build their farms into the rocks, in areas which are unsuitable for cultivating millet anyway.

Years of cultivation have gradually changed the character of the Mandara Mountains. Small terraces have been laid out and cultivated on the steepest slopes of the mountains. These plateaus surrounded by stones are often no bigger than a table and the natural rock structure determines the course of the footpaths leading through them. The caves and caverns of the mountains contain vessels for the souls of the dead and sacrificial altars.

Today granaries, living quarters, kitchens and stables are built according to very rigid traditions. Thus the graves of the ancestors are cylindrical stone-wall constructions, in which the dead are buried facing the compound so that they have constant control over it. The compounds are constructed according to symbols which have been handed down from generation to generation, and often only the elders understand them. The people continue to build according to the same patterns and what has proved useful once is used again and again. The silos of the Mofu are phallic in shape, and there are strict rules for their use. The millet granary of

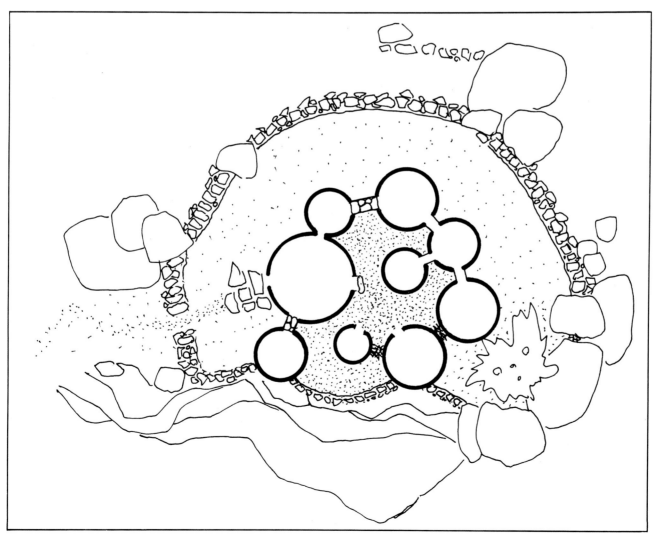

Ground-plan of a Mofu compound in the Mandara Mountains (Cameroon).

Cross-section of a Kirdi farmstead near Mokolo.

the Matakam can only be entered by the men whereas all other granaries can be used by the women as well.

The lay-out of a Kirdi farmstead reflects their social hierarchy. The inner courtyard can only be reached by passing through the house of the *pater familias*. In this way the head of the family can control all comings and goings. Inside, the houses are strictly divided into those allotted to the women, children, animals and those used for the storage of agricultural products. Thus the system within corresponds to the outward form, and the architecture is so well-adapted to the geographical conditions that many farms on the slopes of the mountains seem to be completely absorbed into the surrounding countryside. This is also due to the fact that the walls of the houses are built of stones and clay, and the roofs covered with millet straw.

The architecture of the Musgum, a Kirdi tribe living on the banks of the Logone near Buss, differs greatly from that of any other mountain people. They are masters of expressive architecture and scholars and travellers have always found their dome-like buildings impressive. The clay is pounded; as with other tribes, straw is added, and the material is then made durable with goat's urine. The work is comparable to that of a potter. The domes are built from below without any skeleton, and the outer structure does not only serve to strengthen the building but also proves use-

ful when repairs or redecoration become necessary, or when, during one of the rare downpours of rain, a straw lid has to be put on the circular ventilation-hole. Many years ago travellers discovered Musgum houses up to ten metres high. But the Musgum architects who are still capable of building houses such as these will probably share the fate of other true African architects: They will eventually die, and their knowledge will die with them.

The Architecture of the Dogon

One of the outstanding examples of African architecture is the Dogon village as it is found in the Bandiagara escarpment south of the Great Niger Bend. Here one of the most interesting and diversified architectural conceptions in Africa has been preserved.

Ogol has all the traits of a typical, genuine Dogon village. It is laid out from north to south in the form of a man stretched out on his back. In the diagram the menstruation houses can be seen as the hands while the *Toguna* and the forge represent the head. The homesteads of the families in the centre of the village are the breasts and the stomach; the altars in the south of the village are the feet, and the millstones embody the sex organs in the form of a vagina. The phallic symbols which should have been set up next to them were arranged outside the village walls in deference to the women. Thus the figure of man becomes the religious expression of Dogon architecture.

1 *Toguna* (assembly hall)
2 *Ginna* (homestead of the families)
3 Menstruation houses
4 *Lannea* (millstone)
5 Founding altar
6 Altars

114 (above) Musgum compound in North Cameroon. – 114 (below) Living quarters with stable. The domelike kitchen has an opening for the smoke. The ribbing on the outer walls strengthens the construction.

Family sitting in front of their house in Sirigu (northern Ghana).

Each construction is based on the creation myth, according to which the universe is composed of fourteen spheres. One of them is the earth, which is surrounded by vast expanses of water and embraced by a serpent biting its tail. The earth is believed to be the uppermost of the seven lower discs. Above it there are seven more, each with its own sun and moon. The centre around which the fourteen spheres rotate is called *Ammadyi*, the creator god being *Amma*. *Amma* not only created man but also the fauna, the earth and the moon. His act of creation generated various genii, which influence both the life and architecture of the Dogon. The Dogon believe that they were driven out of the pre-Islamic empire of Mande and then wandered to the Bandiagara region.

117 Steps leading to the mosque of Djenné.

There they came upon a people of small stature whom they still call Pygmies. The Tellem, or "small red people", were bearers of an outstanding culture which, in the course of time, blended with that of the Dogon.

Religion is the key to an understanding of Dogon architecture, for religious motifs pervade their villages and settlements. Apart from a wide range of symbols, which reveal their religious beliefs, there are architectural elements directly embodying the myth. The most important of all buildings in a Dogon village is the *Toguna,* usually a rectangular construction with the outer walls facing the four cardinal points. Eight supporting columns embody the primordial ancestors, four male and four female, who were

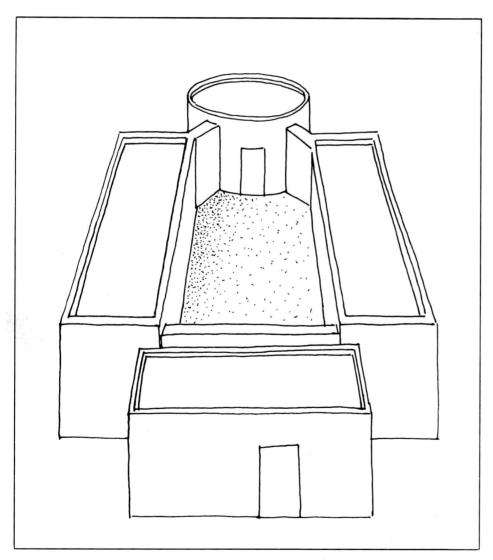

In the village of Banani the homesteads have an anthropomorphic shape. The round kitchen is the head; the storerooms on the long sides of the inner court are the arms, and the hall symbolizes the legs; the main room of the homestead represents the trunk with the entrance as the sex organs.

119 Symbolism, which has its roots in the creation myth, is all-pervasive in Dogon architecture. Granaries, silos and fetish shrines are decorated with reliefs which are consecrated to demons or gods. – **120/121** The *Toguna* is the meeting place of the men. It is thatched with millet grass or rice straw. The anthropomorphic forked columns symbolize the *Lebe,* the primordial ancestors of the Dogon.

The silos and granaries are built into rock niches in order to protect them from the rain.

the sons and daughters of the first two people created by *Amma.* In the *Toguna,* which is generally thatched with millet grass, the meetings of the elders are held, presided over by the village elder, the *Hogon.* Each village has its *Hogon* and its house of assembly. Occasionally penthouses resembling the roof of the *Toguna* are built in exposed places, such as on hills or rocky plateaus. When constructing the main *Toguna,* the Dogon take care to arrange the forked columns supporting the roof in a spiral line winding from northwest to south. This represents the serpent which, in the creation myth, embraces the earth.

The Dogon come to the altars and sacred places of their villages to make sacrifices through which they hope to attain spiritual strength. The altars divide the territory of the Dogon into reli-

Rock paintings in the shelter of Songo (Mali).

gious districts and thus determine the type of architecture surrounding them. The impact of religion is manifest not only in sacred architecture but also in the construction of the homesteads, which have anthropomorphic ground-plans. Each homestead is divided into stables, granaries, living quarters, a hall and an inner courtyard. Looking down on the village from the cliffs, one can easily make out the anthropomorphic shape of the homesteads. The same pattern is repeated in the lay-out of the whole village:

124/125 Ireli, one of the most impressive of all Dogon villages, is situated at the foot of a precipice. The dead are buried in caves high above the village. Only a few are entitled to enter the sacred niches in the rock face. With long ropes the dead are heaved up into the niches, where they are buried along with their masks, which, like the wearer, are mortal. – **126/127** Ruins are never pulled down. The morbid beauty of dilapidated walls is particularly manifest in Banani. – **128** Silos in the plains south of Bandiagara. – **129** The village of Banani.

The architecture of Shanga is different from that of other Dogon villages in that it has smoothly curved lines.

The most important buildings mark the vital spots of the human body.

Dogon architecture is more than a mere expression of beauty. It reflects an ideology, a philosophy of life, which it illustrates. The constructional elements of the granaries symbolize the eight vital organs of *Nommo*, one of the genii created by *Amma*. They resemble the human organs or the stomach of a bird, for *Nommo* is as fast as a bird. The four crossbeams can be compared to the arms and legs of a woman on her back, whereas the roof they support embodies the heavens. Religious symbolism pervades Dogon architecture but is also evident in everyday objects. The grinding stone for the oil-producing fruits symbolizes the female sex organ, whereas the phallic altar in the village centre stands for

The villages in the Bandiagara escarpment are built on natural rock terraces.

the male sex organ. In the lay-out the women's houses mark the breasts; the *Toguna* represents the head, and the three altars with their *Gri-Gri* symbolize the feet.

132 A narrow lane in Shanga. – **133** A Dogon shrine south of Bandiagara; its façade looks like a face. – **134/135** A *Toguna* in the plains south of Bandiagara. – **137** View of Pegue with ancestral burial places and granaries at the foot of the rock face. – **138/139** Rock paintings in the shelter of Songo (Dogon). – **140** Granary (Dogon). – **141** The village of Shanga. – **142** (above) The hunter's house with fetishes. – **142** (below) Houses in Shanga. – **143** An inner courtyard in Shanga. – **144/145** According to Marcel Griaule, the *Ginna,* the house of the *Hogon,* has eight rows of ten niches each, representing the *Lebe,* the eight primordial ancestors with their descendants, who are as numerous as the fingers of both hands. These niches are the final abodes of the ancestors, which they occupy in successive order according to the dates of their birth. The niches should never be walled up because the ancestors need fresh air to breathe. If there are not enough niches, columns are added. Ten swallow's nests are put into the ten round niches at the top because the swallow is the bird of the ancestors. These are called "swallow's niches", a name which, in deference to the ancestors, is used for all the niches in the façade.

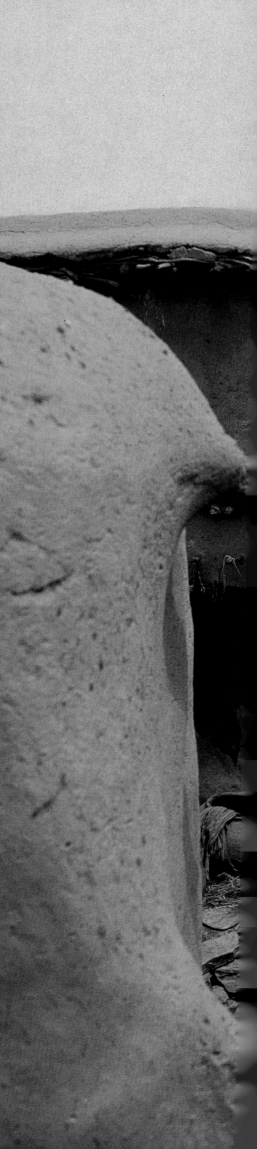

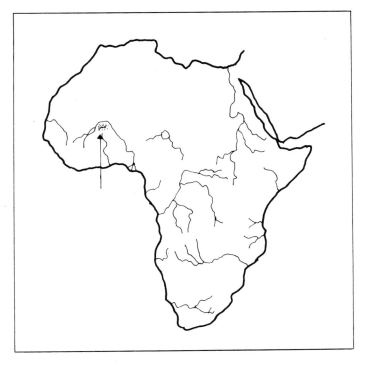

The Dogon

South of the Great Niger Bend there is a mountain range which has been the scene of a fantastic ethnic and cultural evolution for more than 2000 years.

The Falaise de Bandiagara is the home of the Dogon, probably the most interesting people in West Africa. When the first reports from Bandiagara, Shanga and Douentza reached Europe, nobody realized that a spot of such historical importance, the home of one of the eldest black African cultures, had been discovered. In the mid-Seventies a group of Dutch scientists was able to prove that the caves in the Bandiagara escarpment had been inhabited as early as 500 B.C., and that this period saw the birth of a fascinating artistic and cultural era.

The Tellem, a people which lived in the area around Bandiagara before the Dogon, laid the foundation to the form and content of a unique art. The Dogon took over the style and symbolism of this art many years later, after they had driven the Tellem away and settled on their land.

Their mythology, which is described in the chapter on architecture, was the source of an incredible abundance of sacred wood

146 Dogon woman in front of a typical granary. – **148/149** The onion plantations of the Dogon are laid out along the dammed-up stream. The women cut the green of the onions into small pieces and form balls which are part of the food of the Dogon.

carvings, sculptures, masks and ancestral figures. Apart from these works of art, small stones of anthropomorphic form as well as ritual iron staffs bear witness to a highly developed artistic tradition. Religion, which has always influenced the life, architecture, music and dance of the Dogon, inspired them to create sculptures of wood and stone personifying mythological necessities.

The Dogon use a great number of masks, especially for funeral ceremonies, where masks are of the utmost importance. In these rites the masks serve as an abode for the spirits of the dead, thus preventing them from harming the living while they search for a new body.

The most important of these masks is the so-called *Iminana*, or Great Mask. It is shaped like a prostrate serpent with a rectangular head. Sometimes the body of the serpent, which is carved from a flat piece of wood, is ten metres long. The Great Mask commemorates the primordial ancestors of the Dogon. Every sixty years a new *Iminana* is carved and presented to the community in the course of a ceremony which is called *Sigui*. According to the rites each member of the community has to do penance for the primordial ancestor who violated a sacred law. The *Iminana* is their most highly treasured possession and is only used for the *Sigui* ceremony or for the funeral rites of high-ranking personalities. Many Dogon masks also depict animals from their religious mythology. Some groups have their own masks representing their various occupations.

By wearing masks the dancers can give up their identity and assume the symbolic meaning of the mask, which demands that they dance according to a prescribed choreography.

Apart from animal masks there are also masks depicting human beings and expressing their peculiarities or ailments. One of these masks is the *Hogon* mask, which embodies the old man; another is the mask representing the deaf-mute. Occasionally inanimate objects are protrayed. The most impressive of these is the mask of

151 Young Dogon mother. – **152/153** Fetish shrine on the way to Banani.

150

a multistoreyed house. The face of this mask—just like that of the hare mask—resembles the portal of the mosque of Mopti.

The most famous mask is the *Kanaga,* a mask of atonement which represents the *Kanaga* bird and is intended to protect the wearer from the revenge of the slaughtered animal. A head-piece in the form of a modified Cross of Lorraine depicts a deity showing man in the act of creation. One type of mask called *Sigire,* which symbolizes the house of the *Hogon,* the village elder, who is the custodian of tradition, has a superstructure with eighty pierced decorations commemorating the eighty founders of the tribe.

It is obvious that an artist who can build up on a tradition which, in its essence, has remained the same for hundreds of years will be able to create a highly expressive work of art in which he believes and which is an essential part of his life. This alone made it possible for the Dogon to reach a standard which is unrivalled anywhere else.

International trade in works of art and an increasing interest in African art among collectors have largely been responsible for the development of a whole industry around this traditional art which produces imitations of the most interesting items. Many of the Dogon counterfeit works of art themselves and supply the market without considering religious ties or commitments. Only rarely can their products compete with the quality of the original. It would be interesting to discover why the masks a Dogon artist carves for tourist trade are hardly ever convincing. Perhaps it is the deeply rooted piety which is the source for the inimitable expressiveness of these works of art. Perhaps the life of the artist must harmonize with his feelings and thoughts if he is to create a

155–157 The Dogon of Ogol make a sacrifice. When long periods of drought jeopardize the harvest, when there are plagues or when somebody is dying, the inhabitants of Ogol sacrifice a goat. The *Hogon* presides over the ritual and decides who has to make the sacrifice. In this way the Dogon hope to appease their ancestors who will then ask the gods for mercy. Whoever wrongly or carelessly makes a sacrifice exposes himself to the wrath of the spirits who will make him suffer for it. – **158–161** For ritual dances the Dogon use many different masks which represent animals, deities, ancestors or houses. Important times such as the sowing of the seed or the harvesting of millet are initiated by great festivities.

highly expressive work of art. Be that as it may, the younger Dogon generation is no longer able to attain this expressiveness.

Ever since the ethnologists Marcel Griaule and Germaine Dieterlen informed the world about the Dogon people, an increasing interest in Dogon art has gone hand in hand with a deterioration in its quality. Like all other African peoples who have drawn the attention of the outside world, the Dogon have become showmen who seem to hate tourism but are not willing to forego its advantages.

In spite of the fact that Dogon art and traditions are rapidly deteriorating, their architecture has managed to preserve its purity of artistic expression. Tin roofs and concrete walls have not yet spoiled the villages along the Bandiagara Cliffs. South of Bandiagara the architecture of the Dogon has survived unadulterated in more than a hundred villages. Some houses, however, which used to be decorated with works of art have changed in appearance. The carved granary doors decorated with figures of ancestors and animals are all gone, taken away by collectors, dealers and ethnologists who are also responsible for stripping the villages of the anthropomorphic, forked beams of their *Togunas*. The *Togunas* of many villages were removed in the Sixties and since then some have been replaced by new ones of inferior artistic quality. Dozens of figures were simply chopped off the forked beams on the assumption that they would sell more easily than the heavy beams, and this was an act of destruction bordering on vandalism.

The psychiatrist Fritz Morgentaler and Mr. and Mrs. Paris-Mattey describe the Dogon as a frugal, modest people. However, in recent years this can no longer be said of the younger generation. In some villages I met young men who were dissatisfied with their lot. One of them, who had spent two years in the army, said that he did not want to return to his community where life was miserable and opportunities were limited. More and more young Dogon will eventually break with their ethnic background and, by renouncing their home, will hasten the decay of their culture.

Ganvié, the Village on Stilts

Ganvié is not only the largest but also the most beautiful village of lake dwellings in Africa. More than 10,000 people live in this settlement on the shores of Lake Nokwé only a few kilometres north of Cotonou. Unlike most other African lake villages, Ganvié does not only stand in water during the rainy season or when the floods raise the water level of the lagoon, but throughout the year. There were three reasons for the inhabitants of Ganvié, who live exclusively on fishing, to settle in the middle of the lake. Firstly, it is the easiest way for them to reach their fishing grounds. Secondly, the wide reed belt surrounding the lake protects them very effectively from any kind of enemy. And thirdly, paradoxically enough, there are far fewer mosquitoes on the lake than on the swampy shores where these unpleasant insects breed.

Ganvié can only be reached by boat. No dam, no bridge, no footpath connects it with the shore. This may be one of the reasons why ancient craftsmanship, architecture and traditions have been preserved. The dwellings are made in the same manner as they were made in the middle of the last century when Ganvié was founded: The fishermen use beams and ribs of palm branches, which they tie into the roofs. The houses, which resemble prehistoric lake dwellings, are covered with thick thatched roofs. Only the Christian church disturbs the harmony of the scene.

With its brick walls and shiny, corrugated roof it interferes with the cultural backround of this village, the inhabitants of which are members of the predominantly animistic Fon tribe. The walls of the houses are covered with fetishes, earthenware vessels containing essences and elixirs, magic objects and sacrificial altars. Few villages in Africa have been changed by tourism to such a degree as has Ganvié, and only in the last couple of years have measures been taken to get the situation under control. High entrance fees and scheduled sightseeing tours have been introduced, and although this creates a rather uniform and an all too rigid atmosphere, the Ganvié of today is more pleasant than it was, for, in spite of its picturesque beauty, it used to be one of the worst places for visitors in the whole of Africa. Women, children, beggars and profiteers, all yelling for money, used to harass every tourist passing through the village. The tourists reaped the harvest they had themselves sown: ignorance, arrogance and a lack of respect for everything belonging to a different culture.

Like the inhabitants of the coast, the fishermen of Ganvié have formed communes and have built weirs by driving hundreds of stakes and branches into the bottom of the lake. Every day they set out for the fishing grounds with nets they cast standing either in their boats or in the water.

When in the late afternoon the boats take the last Europeans out of the village, the atmosphere on the lake changes. Smoke rises from the thatched roofs; baskets full of small fish are unloaded from the fishing boats and are grilled over the fires of the small clay ovens which can be found in almost every hut. In this way the main food of the inhabitants of Ganvié is preserved for a whole week. On the next morning the women take the smoke-dried fish to the market and trade them for manioc, yams or millet. Compared with the work it entails, the amount of fish caught is usually rather small, and only the frugality of the people makes it possible for them to lead this modest life on Lake Nokwé.

164 Lake-dwellings in the process of being built. – **166–171** Scenes at the lake-dwellings of Ganvié.

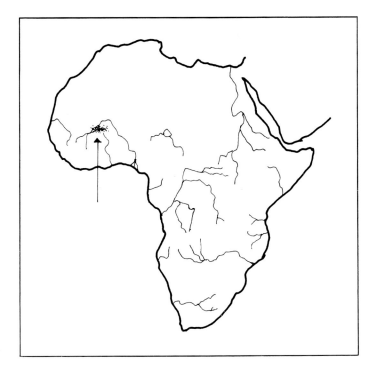

The Peul

In the opinion of the Peul of Djenné it is a bad omen if the storks arrive early. It signifies that the rainy season will start earlier than usual and that the rain, which thus falls on the cracked clay crusts of the parched marshes, will be missing when the flood waters of the Niger are expected and needed every year to submerge the basin. After the long droughts of the Seventies this lush grassland was overgrazed to such a degree that it lost its former function as an enormous water-absorbing sponge. In this way the floods reached the town of Gao earlier than in previous years because the vast belt of vegetation along the Niger which had prevented the waters from draining off before had gone.

When the rains begin, the Niger Basin turns into a gigantic lake. Thousands of pirogues cross the waters and the activity on the swamps between Djenné and Timbuktu reaches a climax. In former times when these two places were still the cultural centres of the Sahel a fleet of boats secured brisk trade of goods in both directions. Islamic learning and scholarship formed the background for the close business relations which were kept up for centuries by the caravans in the north and the river boats in the south. This

172 Peul woman at the market of Djenné. – 174/175 Market day in Djenné, with a view of the mosque. – 177 Peul market woman. – 178/179 The women bring the milk for sale in calabashes. – 180/181 Market day in Djenné.

area south of the Great Niger Bend was later invaded by the Peul, a nomadic pastoral people who in Niger and Cameroon are called the Bororo. The Peul or Fulbe tribes are of the same origin but have different ways of life. Some of them have become sedentary while others still pursue their nomadic life. The differences between the various tribes are manifest in their clothing, their jewelry and their culture. Some traits, however, are common to all of them, namely their arrogance, devotion to their herds and aggressiveness towards their neighbours. The Songhai, the Bozo as well as the Dogon and the Tuareg accuse them of haughtiness and quarrelsomeness. The journalist Georg Gerster told of embittered conflicts between the Peul and other tribes which arose when the cowherds recklessly drove their cattle through newly cultivated plantations.

A couple of years ago the government forced the Peul to confine their wanderings to certain routes, which was of course a bitter pill for these freedom-loving nomads to swallow, all the more so as there was a general trend towards restricting their movements anyway. In the meantime, however, the government has had to realize that nomadism ensures the most effective utilization of grazing land.

The Peul of Djenné have preserved some elements of matriarchy which give the women economic independence. Every woman and even every child has his or her own herd, and this makes it possible for them to lead an individual life outside the limits of a restrictive hierarchy.

Thus it may be easier to understand that ideological and social discrepancies between the Peul and their neighbours are a source of continual conflict. The division of most black African tribes into age groups and families with their strict laws is a challenge to the independent, freedom-loving Peul. This does not mean that they do not have any traditions themselves, but theirs seem to be different and more tolerant.

183 Peul woman from Upper Volta. – 184/185 Wedding celebrations among the Peul of Upper Volta.

Every monday Djenné is the scene of a colourful gathering of people in bright clothes. The market place is a turmoil of yelling, laughing and haggling dealers and customers jostling one another. Here the Bozo meet the unpopular Peul, the Bambara and the Tuareg. All of them are eager to sell their goods before nightfall; otherwise they have to take them home again. They have long distances to cover on foot or on the back of a donkey. Many use lorries to get to the river through which they wade with their wares on their heads. In front of the splendid mosque activity begins in the early morning.

Although the Peul are all of the same origin, they are a heterogeneous people. The Peul south of Bandiagara, for instance, lead a poorer life than those on the marshes along the Niger. Their jewelry is less precious and their clothing is as simple as their lives. From time to time migrant bards, or Griots, pass by and sing of the latest news and of war heroes of long ago. They tell of girls and women. The texts chanted to the sound of a single-stringed guitar, always have a grain of wisdom. Such customs are stronger among the Peul than among other tribes because they belong to the most gifted musicians and singers of Africa.

The daily life of these nomads is completely different from that of the Dogon in the north. Nevertheless, a certain degree of tolerance and mutual acceptance have made it possible for such disparate groups to co-exist. The Dogon find the Peul women more attractive than their own, and many intermarriages work without any problems. On the other hand the Peul greatly appreciate the skill of the Dogon in sinking a new well. These people have a lot in common, and in recent years it has become natural for the Peul to set up their camps near the Dogon villages or even make their homes in them. As nomads, the Peul have many neighbours, for they constantly come into contact with various other peoples. However, they have retained their characteristic way of life.

186 Peul mother with child. – **188/189** Peul girl doing the housework. – **190/191** Peul children weaving bast plates.

The Lobi

The corner of land between the states of Ghana, Upper Volta and the Ivory Coast is the home of the Lobi. Particularly in recent years this tribe has begun to attract the attention of European and American collectors who have discovered the value of its creative art. Today the Lobi are farmers and cattle-breeders, but in the past they were also hunters and fishermen, particularly on the banks of the Volta River. Many rituals still practised today come from that period. Water gods play an important part in their life, and every seven years the former fishermen celebrate the *Dyoro* festival, using a clay figure to symbolize the Volta.

The statues of the Lobi are usually protective fetishes. The effigies often have helmet-like headgears and are striking for their exquisitely carved faces. The Lobi are not only excellent wood-carvers but also blacksmiths who are masters of lost wax casting. The Ashanti taught them the art of casting iron, which the Lobi, in performing their religious duties, have perfected.

The architecture of the Lobi is the most conspicuous feature for the traveller. There are a lot of striking similarities between the architectural styles of the Lobi and the Somba-Tamberma, who also build protective constructions in the form of castle-like

192 Dilapidated Lobi farm. – 194/195 Lobi woman with her children in front of the central granary. – 196 Every Lobi farm has its own altar. – 197 Cooking at a traditional Lobi farm.

houses with high windowless outer walls. Today these houses are made of clay whereas, in the past, stone was the principle building material. By glazing the fragile clay façades with the milky sap of plants, the Lobi enhance the solidity of the outer walls. Similar techniques are used for the construction of houses among the Bassari in Togo and in northern Ghana. The Lobi villages consist of clay houses with flat, terraced roofs. The architectural style varies from tribe to tribe. The roofs, which are supported by forked beams, are usually reinforced with rafters and branches. The homesteads of the Lobi are completely roofed-in compounds dominated by the granary. As soon as this square store-house has been completed, the other units of the compound are added.

As head of the compound, the father of the family is the one responsible to the elders or to the government. Herta Haselberger reports that the distance between compounds is at least a hundred metres in length. This indicates that the protection of the personal sphere is essential to the African peoples, particularly the Lobi, Somba and other agricultural tribes of the savanna. The uniformity of the settlements reflects the equal social status of all men at the head of a family. Thus one compound rarely outdoes another in size or equipment and decoration.

The importance of the world of spirits, so deeply rooted in West African culture becomes evident in the construction of the houses. Altars are set up within the walls and in the outer courts. The head of the compound is both priest and custodian of the family and ancestral altars. He alone is authorized to make sacrifices or to permit sacrifices to be made by other members of the family. Some altars are set up by individuals for self-preservation. Private altars can even be found on the roofs of houses and in the fields. These altars house supernatural spirits, and sacrifices have to be made on them to preserve and increase their power. Ancestral altars are considered the meeting places of the spirits or Pandemonia where ritual petitions can be made.

199 A Lobi farmhouse. The walls are high and windowless, and the clay façades are glazed with the milky sap of plants to increase the solidity of the outer walls.

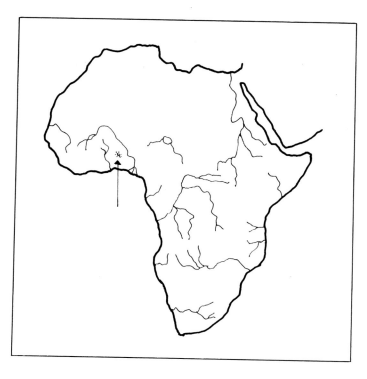

The Somba

In Europe little more is known about the Somba than that the men wear penis sheaths to protect their genitals in the traditional whip fights and that the women and children run around almost naked, their only adornment being delicate chains and strips of kid leather.

Today, however, this paradisiac state of innocence has disappeared. The children hang about the roads begging, and angrily scolding women hide themselves from the glances of strangers. Whenever a European wants to take a picture, crowds of Somba immediately involve him in an angry dispute wanting him to give them a present, a "cadeau".

200 Phallic symbols mark the burial places of the Somba. They are doused with millet beer, all kinds of food and the blood of sacrifical animals. Only certain persons, usually the elder of the clan or the head of the family, are enitled to make sacrifices. Among the Somba, scarifications of the skin are not only body decoration. They are arranged in such a way as to prevent demons or spirits from taking possession of the body. They are a magic protection against evil spirits, which threaten the lives of the living. – **202/203** In most West African tribes and in particular in tribes with a negroid cultural heritage, the worship of the dead has a strong influence on the architecture of the houses. It is believed that the dead are cohabitants, and this belief is reflected in the construction of the houses. That is why the Somba have altars and fetishes consecrated to their ancestors both inside and outside their houses. – **204/205** The whip fight is one of the most important traditions of the Somba. As part of the initiation rites young men are whipped but they are not allowed to show any signs of pain. On other occasions whip fights are held like battles or duels. – **206** Somba homestead with a roofless granary.

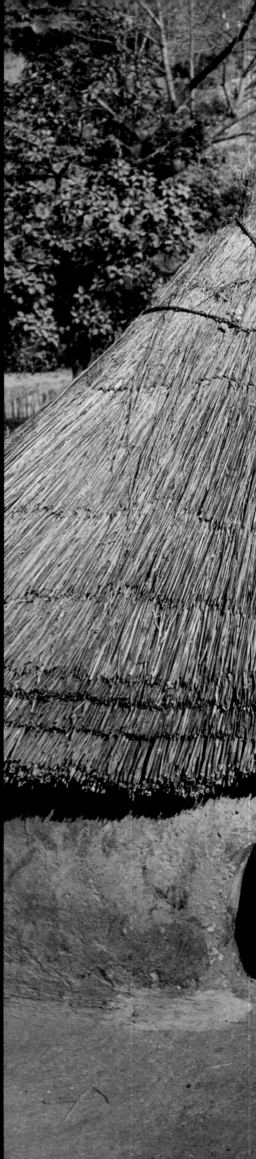

Several years ago the country of the Somba presented a completely different picture. Then, it was an impassable region interspersed with the typical castles of the Somba, with millet fields and plantations which grew so exuberantly during the rainy season that the villages disappeared beneath the plants and the area seemed to be uninhabited. The children and women were shy and afraid of strangers, who were only approached by the men.

The Somba, whose settlements reach far into Dahomey, have always been difficult, for they are a stubborn, self-willed mountain people adhering to their traditions and not afraid to offer resistance, not even to the colonial powers. During the long rainy seasons their country used to be inaccessible so that they could live off the beaten track according to their own indigenous laws.

Today the country of the Somba has changed. Ever since the hotel industry, run by the government of Togo, has started to swamp the area regularly with tourists, an alarming degeneration in manners and mores has taken place among the Somba in the same way as among the Kirdi of Cameroon and the Dogon of Mali. The Somba have exchanged their nakedness for ridiculous rags which generous travellers have given them in exchange for quivers and arrows. They have marketed their hospitality by demanding set prices for the visit to a tribal home or for the permission to take pictures. Their magnificent architecture has been adulterated by strange outbuildings, which usually serve as accommodation for adolescents. The increasing density of the population in some areas, a result of government policy, is changing the character of the country from year to year.

207 P. Mercier describes the architecture of the Somba-Tamberma as follows: "The castle-like buildings of this people reflect the great antagonisms of the cosmos. The terrace, representing the world of the living, is set against the basement, the realm of the dead. The righthand part of the house is reserved for the men, whereas the left is the section for the women and for the female in general. Somba castles are built in various styles. Most homesteads have flat, terrace-like roofs whereas some are covered with conical thatched roofs. In the opinion of Herta Haselberger, the former type, which can also be found among some Tayaba tribes at the foot of the Attacora Mountains southwest of Tanguiéta, is the older one. In such homesteads the women and children sleep on the roof and consequently everyone leaving the house has to pass through the father's room, which makes it easy for him to supervise the family."

The architecture of the Somba has always attracted the attention of travellers. Their castle-like homesteads consist of stables, the granary, the kitchen and living quarters. A special place is reserved for the altar on which regular offerings of millet gruel are made. Outside the homesteads a number of consecrated places are marked by phallic symbols, sacrificial vessels and carcasses of dead animals. The burial places, which are always close to the houses, bear a striking resemblance to those of the Lobi. The walls of the houses are made of mud, which is put on in layers and mixed with straw in order to increase the solidity. The roofs, supported by forked beams, are reinforced with branches. The terraces are then used to dry millet and other agricultural products. To reach their sleeping place the women and children have to climb the roof and crawl through small apertures. In the traditional Somba regions the castles stand far apart from one another because of the size of the fields, the concept of possession and, above all, the marked individualism of the Somba.

Compared with other tribes, the culture of the Somba is not very rich in artistic expression. They play flutes and decorate their quivers and hunting weapons. During the harvest festival, groups of people move from homestead to homestead and are given food for their performances.

The Somba initiation rites are uncommonly cruel. The young men to be initiated undergo a ritual whipping during which they are not allowed to show signs of pain or fear. Only then are they acknowledged as adults and warriors. Whoever fails to endure the ordeal is stigmatized as a coward for the rest of his life. Long scars on the backs of the men are proof of the whip fights which take place on other occasions as well. Every three years self-appointed opponents fight each other to prove their courage again. When asked whether the whipping was painful, one of the fighters (see illustration) said he felt nothing because the fight was a ritual which made him insensible to pain. This was due to the trancelike state of the fighters, who use stimulating drinks and invoke the gods while preparing for the ritual.

Ewe fetish priest of Aflao.

The Somba of Togo call themselves Tamberma and insist on the name being used because they know that, in the language of their neighbours, the word Somba means naked, and nakedness is something derogatory. Again an ethnic name, originally intended as a word of abuse, has continued to be used. Kirdi and Habbe, coined by the Fula, meant pagan or godless, savage or yokel. Today the Somba refuse to be yokels any longer and wear clothes. They cover their nakedness with junk bought from tourists. In tattered raincoats and flowered bras they stand at the roadside begging and grabbing for money. The Somba are another African people bearing the stigma of an alien civilization and inundated with transistor radios, plastic shoes and promises of happiness. 210

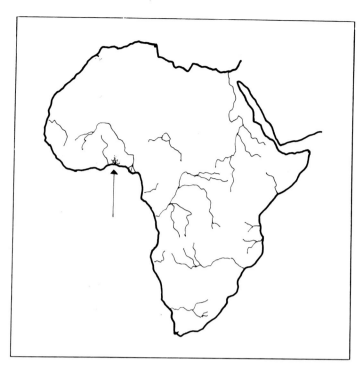

The Ewe

In one respect the Ewe, who live in southern Togo and Ghana, are different from all other tribes described in this book: most of them have been urbanized in recent years and have adopted a way of life influenced to a large extent by European values. Strictly speaking, they no longer belong to the "last Africans" who have retained their natural way of life and still adhere to their traditional heritage. Nevertheless, I have included them in this book because they have retained strong and vital traditions in their religious beliefs. In Togo the Ewe outnumber all other ethnic groups. The coastal areas are populated by the Ewe, the Minah and the Watshi who are all fishermen and farmers. Despite the Catholic Missionary Society of Lyons, which started its activities in Togo before 1884 and intensified them because of an initiative on the part of the North German Protestant Mission in 1914, most of the tribes in Togo still have their traditional animistic beliefs, which have remained the dominant religious force. Islam, which gradually spread from the north, not only came to predominate the towns of Sokodé and Lama-Kara but it also exerted an increasing influence in northern Togo.

212–215 Fetish market in Lomé. – 216 Ewe fetish in Lomé with sacrifices. – 217 Ewe girl with the puppets of her dead brothers and sisters. – 218/219 Fetish priest in Lomé. – 220–224 *Voodoo* ritual performed in a village on the shores of Lake Togo.

As in most other countries of Africa, various Christian churches such as Jehovah's Witnesses, Anglicans and Methodists have gained a footing in Togo. The latest mission to be established was the Baptist Missionary Association of America, which concentrates its activities on the north of the country.

This brief survey is intended to throw light on the situation of the Ewe, who are the target of all these missionary endeavours. According to statistical data collected by Josef Schramm, the Catholic mission has been the most successful of the Christian denominations. The North German Missionary Society, which emphasizes in two of its statutes "that the denominational conflicts rooted in our history must not be taken into the pagan world", has also launched activities which were a "blessing" for Togo.

Finally, however, the denominational conflicts were taken into the pagan world after all, and throughout Africa there is evidence of the hostility which the Christian churches have stirred up in their struggle for African souls. Although the Ewe, like the other forty-one ethnic groups of Togo, have stood in the crossfire of churches and sects from all over the world, most of them still adhere to their traditional religious beliefs.

In all black African countries animistic beliefs and primitive religions are based on the same fundamental conceptions. One deity is commonly worshipped as the creator god whereas lesser deities, demons or genii serve as intermediaries between the living and the creator god. In this connection ancestor worship is essential because those in distress can only reach their god through the mediation of their ancestors, who are able to establish communication with the deities and spirits.

In Africa, old people have a special social status largely because they are closer to death than anyone else, and because on the day of their death they will set out on a journey which will take them to the gods. In their wrath they would wreak vengeance on the living so that it is important to try and win their favour. The social behaviour of the Ewe is governed by this devotion to the old and their pronounced sense of solidarity within the family. The family

225

is more important than anything else, and the clan decides the fate of the individual.

The Anlo-Ewe worship a god they call *Mawu*. He is the creator god who is believed to love the contemplative rather than the masses. Legend has it that *Mawu* left the earth he had created because man demanded too much of him. A number of lesser gods, the so-called *Trowo,* derive their power from *Mawu.* They embody rivers, plants, lagoons and animals. Fetishes are dedicated to them to put them into a benevolent mood.

Pierre Kofi, a converted Christian who works for the tourist office in Lomé, is a member of the Ewe tribe. After years of study in Germany he now lives in Togo and earns his living as an interpreter and expert on tourism. One day Pierre visited his father in Anécho, who told him that he had consulted the oracle and learnt that his son's life was in danger. Pierre himself then consulted a fetish priest of the Minah, who advised him to have two cuts made into his chest which would help to ward off dangers.

Like the Minah, the Ewe have fetish shrines in which fetish priests carry out various kinds of therapy. Studies have shown that, particularly in cases of mental disorders or psychosomatic diseases, the practices of witch doctors yield better results than the therapy used in European hospitals. The treatment is often lengthy and the patients are sometimes interned for months. They are compelled to live according to the strict orders of the fetish priest. These include dietary restrictions, fasting days and other practices which in fact are not unknown to the Christian church. Silence for long periods and sacrificial offerings are demanded of the patients. Occasionally the witch doctor also prescribes shock therapy, for example the strangling and sacrificing of one's own dog, which is part of the initiation rites of the Somba.

Since modern psychology makes use of similar methods, it is strange that the successes of the fetish priests have persistently been denied recognition. Even Albert Schweitzer, who went to

Ghana as a Christian and a doctor, could not avoid putting the animistic witch doctor Michel of Aponge in charge of certain diseases which are rooted in the psyche.

The continuous impact of Christian and Muslim churches has also had its effect on the primitive religions. There are among the Ewe a number of fetish priests who have devoted themselves to a kind of *Voodoo* cult. The *Voodoo* cult, which spread from Dahomey to the American continent, originated in the religion of the Yoruba. As in South America, various primitive religions in Africa assimilated Christian elements and the synthesis created new religious beliefs. Among the Ewe of Lomé, all these blends of religion can be found in an amazing variety. The peoples of south Togo are strongly influenced by the culture of the Yoruba whose religions and traditions have retained their original strength to such a degree that they have had a tremendous impact on other peoples. The Ewe have taken over the custom of making puppets for the dead, which originally came from the *Ibedji* twin puppets of the Yoruba. When a child dies, it is replaced by a wooden puppet, which then houses the spirit of the child. These puppets are carefully dressed, washed and fed because they are considered to be identical with the dead person. The Ifa oracle is also known to the Ewe in a modified form, and each village has its elder who knows how to interpret it.

Another cult which has many parallels with *Voodoo* is frequently practised in Lomé. The fetish priest places a chosen person in the middle of a circle (see illustrations). This person has to hold a bowl filled with water in his hands, and the priest or priestess puts herbs and fragrant essences into the bowl. The invocation of the spirits which follows is accompanied by constant chanting. While kaolin powder and perfumes are being rubbed into the head of the chosen person, the circle of dancers works itself up into ecstasy. If he shows no reaction, someone cuts the throat of a fowl and spills the blood over his head and chest. After a while he begins, slightly bent over backwards, to imitate the movements of the dancers and his facial expression changes. His eyes begin to rotate until he finally starts a wild dance spilling the water around him. At the end of the dance, which he performs in a trance-like state, he collapses in complete exhaustion. The purpose of this ritual is to reach a state in which the person or the patient is able to establish contact with the world of the spirits thereby reducing his psychological tension. In all the exorcisms I have witnessed this aim was reached, however, only among those natives who knew the purpose of the ritual and who were endowed by nature with a higher sensibility for metaphysical phenomena.

The Ewe have a vivid metaphysical imagination. Unaffected by technical progress and alien civilizations, the world of the spirits has remained a vital force for the majority of the population. This may explain why a fetish market unparalleled on the African continent has survived in the middle of the modern metropolis of Lomé. Here fetish priests and patients can find every object and every medicine imaginable. The objects offered for sale include carcasses of birds, heads of monkeys, toads and chameleons, a large selection of bones, tortoise-shells and dog's teeth, strangely shaped ritual iron staffs, which are driven into the earth to appease the earth spritis, and also skins, hides and half-rotten owls, which are used as protection against evil spritis. Although in general the Ewe are not very prolific in producing works of art, they do carve small fetishes, which are not only used for the treatment of mental disorders but also to make all sorts of dreams come true. These small figures are usually tied together, back to back, equipped with flasks of medicine and doused with blood before they are offered for sale. The most typical of these are the twin figures where the one has a cork in its ear and the other one in its mouth. When the first figure is uncorked, it is ready to hear a question while the second will give the answer as soon as its mouth is uncorked.

The fetish altars of the Ewe are usually covered with blood, the feathers of fowls and all sorts of whisky and scent bottles. To Africans it is immaterial which object becomes the *Gri-Gri*, for the criterion is not the form but the essence. Thus the Africans attach a significance to the most trivial objects which appears strange to Europeans because they only perceive the form. In the choice of fetishes, aesthetic criteria are unimportant and the material value of the object, its shape and appearance are completely irrelevant. To be able to understand this, foreigners must change their attitude completely, for Europeans in particular find it hard to imagine a discarded plastic doll becoming an object of magic power. The use of carcasses seems more plausible, for it is understandable that the chameleon's strange behaviour must impress and bewilder simple, natural people, who expect even the impaled carcass of a chameleon to radiate demonic power.

In the villages along the coast a different type of *Gri-Gri* is used. Small hemispheres of mud or concrete symbolize heads, their eyes marked with kaori. Sometimes whole rows of them lie along the walls of the houses. These spritis are made by the members of the family, each his own *Gri-Gri* to which he offers sacrifices. Illnesses and family problems are occasions for such rituals. If a member of the family is taken ill, the father makes a sacrifice to the gods. First he pours food, palm wine, oil and millet gruel, over the *Gri-Gri* at the same time invoking the demons and spirits to pass on his supplications to the gods. Then he cuts the throat of a sacrificial fowl and, holding the bleeding animal over his *Gri-Gri,* he again calls for help.

In various villages on the shores of Lake Togo, collective sacrifices are made in which up to fifty people take part and scores of animals are sacrificed. Goats, fowl, dogs and cats are used. These ancient rites are very much alive especially in the villages around Anécho. As in other Ewe and Minah regions, gigantic phallic symbols flank the exits and entrances to the villages. They are protective devices to ward off mischief and disaster.

For many African peoples scarifications, often wrongly interpreted as body decoration, are ritual symbols. The Ewe cut a wedge-shaped scar-line between the shoulder-blades of bare-breasted girls wearing white loincloths. Others are added as required by the ritual. Scarifications may serve as tribal markings.

230

The Karamojong use them to indicate rank. The Fon attribute magical powers to them, and some tribes use them to heighten their erotic appeal. The vanity of the men, which in Africa often exceeds that of the women, has also devised a variety of body tattooing which functions as decoration or substitute for jewelry. The Ikela cut intricate decorations into their skin whereas the Mayumbe adorn their bodies with deep cuts forming large ornamental patterns.

Among the tribes using scarification, the Fon of Dahomey, neighbours to the Ewe, stand out for their virtuosity. The Ewe have adopted their technique. Somewhere on the shores of Lake Togo I was told that scarification need not be done by a fetish priest. In every family one member is a master of the art.

Boris de Rachewiltz tells of the Ewe performing rituals where virgins are consecrated to a snake deity. The hierogamy is enacted by a priest. These orgiastic ceremonies take place when the barley begins to sprout. The fertility rites of the Ewe are closely connected with prostitution. The sacred prostitutes, the *Kosi*, once played an important role in the religion. Today, however, they have virtually disappeared. Profane prostituion has become widespread, superseding the traditional sacred form. Initiation rites have lost most of their meaning. Now, only boys are circumcised in ceremonies which have a lot in common with phallic cults. For some dances the women tie huge wooden phallic symbols to their hips so that with certain movements the phallus is erected. The dancers, who are usually advanced in years, then simulate a coitus. The spectators and dancers burst into laughter when the women pretend to copulate.

Like the Ewe of Togo, the Anlo-Ewe have been living on the shores of Keta Lagoon in southeast Ghana since the seventeenth century. As there are no records, the origin of the Anlo-Ewe has remained obscure. Some historians assume that one of the main groups reached Ghana form the border area between Dahomey and Nigeria. Another group probably settled in Central Togo before the seventeenth century.

231

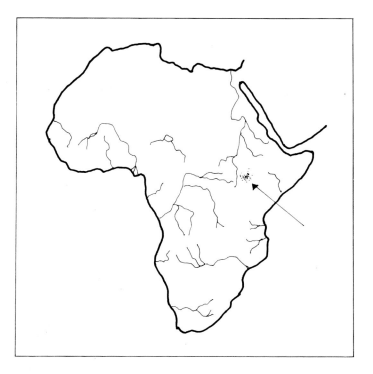

The Karamojong

Even in the colonial era, the Karamojong were known to be a difficult people to handle. They were notorious for their controversies and armed conflicts with neighbouring tribes. They live in the savannas of northern Uganda, where the poor vegetation barely suffices to feed their herds. Although the problems and the way of life of the seven tribes, into which the Karamojong are divided, are similar, they do not get on with one another because their wanderings often lead them into territories claimed by other Karamojong. Frequently this results in open hostilities. The colonial government tried to put an end to these conflicts by dividing the territory among the tribes according to criteria which they thought to be just. The Karamojong, however, refused to observe these borders. In 1958 an agronomist discovered the reason for their apparently unreasonable behaviour. He found that the land within the borders was so poor in minerals that the grass did not have enough nourishment for the cattle. The Karamojong have known this for centuries. Such seemingly insignificant facts, which are incomprehensible to Europeans, are often the key to an understanding of the behaviour of peoples.

232 Daughter of a Karamojong chief. – 234–236 Pastoral family near Moroto (Uganda). – 237 The scars on the shoulder of this Karamojong warrior show the number of enemies he has killed.

Similar to the Peul of West Africa, the Karamojong are closely bound to their herds. Their prestige depends on the number of animals they possess. Their laws have their origin in their way of life. It is therefore hardly surprising that, like elsewhere in Africa, European officials have failed to understand the way of life and problems of the Karamojong. Basil Davidson reports that the colonial government tried to prevent overgrazing and conflicts between neighbouring tribes by passing resolutions aiming at reducing the number of cattle. The number of "authorized" cattle was estimated according to the needs and density of the population. Once again crucial factors were simply ignored. No attention was paid to the fact that during the dry season cattle produce only a fraction of the milk which can be gained during the rainy season. The Karamojong also tap the arteries of their cattle and drink their blood, for they know that during the rainy season three and a half litres of blood can be taken from a fully grown cow without endangering its life. During the dry season, however, one litre could already be fatal. The Karamojong wanted to determine the number of cattle themselves, for they alone knew how many they needed to survive the dry season.

The herds are the means of existence for the animal-loving Karamojong, who depend on them for their prosperity. They are the object of all festivities. They give their names to the male offspring of the tribe. When a Karamojong dies, he is sewn into a cowhide and buried near the kraal. Thus he can reach his god Akuj. Moral values are determined by the needs of the cattle: a Karamojong is prepared to risk his life for his herds and will kill anyone disputing his right to pasture land. His life is marked by extremely harsh conditions, privation and a rigorous hierarchy within age groups. The Tobosa, Dodoth, Teso and Jie or Jye are sub-tribes of the Karamojong with very similar customs and traditions. They distinguish six age groups of which the older ones are superior in rank. These age groups provide the guidelines for their strictly organized way of life and the individual has to behave according to his rank. Anyone appropriating the attributes of superior age groups, dressing improperly or misbehaving himself, is punished.

J. V. Blumenthal reports of a place in Apule which is reserved for exceptional ceremonies. Every thirty years the tribal power is handed over to the next age group. During the ceremony the elders are urged to yield their power to their successors. This ceremony of succession is one of the most important and most sacred events in the lives of the Karamojong. From afar silent processions of cowherds move toward Apule and when they return two weeks later the power has changed hands.

When they marry, the Karamojong take a bride from another clan. Engagements between children occur occasionally. A grown-up bride follows her husband who pays her family a price for her. This varies between three and ten head of cattle; occasionally sheep are also accepted. If the wife dies childless, her husband has no right to reclaim the bride-price. If she is unfaithful or runs away, the clan has to pay back the price paid for her.

These ancient traditions have helped the tribe to survive, and although the severity with which they fight their enemies is sometimes hard to understand, it is natural in a people struggling for mere survival. For centuries the Karamojong have known droughts and cattle plague. Their prosperity is made or marred by the welfare of their cattle. The rolling savannas demand all their strength. Only by continuously migrating and persistently searching for new watering places and new pasture land are they able to keep their herds alive. The government of Uganda is at war with the Karamojong because, like the Kirdi of Cameroon, they are not willing to serve in the army and this has, led to internal conflicts. But time will solve this problem as well.

The first portable radios have reached Karamoja; missionaries of various churches, bent on spreading the blessings of civilization, travel through the country. Soon the Karamojong will be going to school and learning to meet the demands of civilization. Before long they will be joining the army and selling off their herds in order to become industrial workers in the cities.

Short Survey of the Peoples described in this Book

Kirdi A mountain people living in northern Cameroon. Fula slave hunters drove them back into the mountains, where they became millet farmers and cattle-breeders on a small scale. In the Fula language, the word Kirdi means "the godless one" and is intended to be a term of abuse. Centuries of hostilities have turned them into a belligerent people. Their reserve and their seclusion made it possible for them to retain their independence. In the last couple of years tourism has reached northern Cameroon and has begun its work of destruction. The government has forced the Kirdi to wear clothes, thus fundamentally changing the outward appearance of these people. The women have exchanged their traditional bronze jewelry for coloured bras, and skirts, which were bartered from the tourists for shields or spears, have taken the place of the indigenous "Cache-Sex".

Ashanti An important people of the Akan group with a partly matriarchal organization. They live predominantly on agricultural products. Their home is the richly forested southern uplands of Ghana. In the nineteenth century the Ashanti set up a confederate empire. It is ruled over by a king, the so-called Ashantehene, whose residence is the historic town of Kumasi. In the course of history they have developed great skill in lost wax casting, a technique which has been taken over by other tribes.

Bororo A subgroup of the Fula. They are a nomadic people living in Niger, Chad and Cameroon. The Bororo are cattle-breeders who live on trade with their neighbours by exchanging their dairy produce and meat for other products. They are a people of obscure and controversial origin. One theory postulates that they came from the Asian continent and on their migrations mingled with the Berbers of the northern Sahara.

Dogon They live in Mali, in villages along the Bandiagara escarpment. The Dogon are farmers whose main produce is millet. The research of Marcel Griaule has caused their phantastic art und architecture to become the subject of intensive study and has drawn the attention of the whole world. The close interrelation between their architecture and mythology is unique. Their religion, which, like all primitive African religions, is based on ancestor worship, has been the source of great works of art. They seem to have taken over the style of their statues and ancestral figures from the Tellem, a mysterious people who inhabited the Bandiagara escarpment before the Dogon.

Peul A nomadic people of the Sahel region consisting of several sub-tribes, which in recent years have split into two camps. On the one hand, there are those who continue to lead their nomadic life; on the other, there are those who have become sedentary. The Peul have an intense and ardent love for their herds and their families. The vast savannas of the Sahel region are their natural environment. Recent government projects aim at restricting their freedom of movement, which is tantamount to the destruction of the unique nature of this people.

Lobi They are planters who formerly lived off fishing and hunting on the banks of the Volta. Lobi architecture is particularly interesting with its castle-like houses and flat roofs used for drying agricultural products. The Lobi are famous for their wood-carving. Their ancestral altars and fetishes are still designed from ancient models.

Somba Farmers in the savannas of northern Togo and Dahomey (Benin). Their castle-like homes, closed and windowless compounds outwardly resembling fortresses, are particularly impressive. The religion of the Somba is strongly influenced by ancestor worship. Offerings of animals or food on the altars within or outside the houses are intendend to placate the ancestors, spirits and gods. Modernization and technology are contributing to the disintegration of the Somba culture. The government has placed restrictions on the construction of Somba "castles" and has applied other sanctions to integrate the obstinate Somba into the civilized life of neighbouring tribes.

Ewe A people living on the coast of Togo and Ghana, remarkable for their strong ties and traditions. Fishing is the main occupation of the Ewe. They are also planters and farmers. The radical urbanization of the coastal areas in recent years has gone hand in hand with a degeneration in their indigenous way of life. More and more of the Ewe are abandoning their religious practices.

Karamojong Cattle-breeders in northern Uganda. Their living conditions are extremely difficult. Their struggle for survival and the lack of pasture have made them a belligerent people. Their lives, like those of the Bororo, are devoted to their animals. The rythm of their existence is dominated by the needs of their herds. Their festivities and their wanderings are subject to strict rules. The community is divided into age groups, which still exert a strong influence.